# CUT OFF

## BOUNDARIES, ENTITLEMENT, ESTRANGEMENT, AND THE BREAKDOWN OF FAMILY ACCOUNTABILITY

# VENUS CHANDLER

©Copyright 2026

IBG Publications, Inc.

# VENUS CHANDLER

**IBG**
PUBLICATIONS
Putting the POWER in your pen!

Published by I.B.G. Publications, Inc., a Power to Wealth Company

Web address: www.ibgpublications.com

admin@ibgpublications.com / 904-419-9810

Copyright, 2026 by Venus Chandler

IBG Publications, Inc., Jacksonville, FL

ISBN: 978-1-956266-99-3

Chandler, Venus
Cut Off: Boundaries, Entitlement, Estrangement And The Breakdown Of Family Accountability.

Printed in the United States of America.

# DEDICATION

*To my Aunt Ivy:*

My steady ground.
My truth teller.
My unpaid therapist.

When my world fractured in ways I could not yet understand, you stayed. When the pain of being estranged from my children felt unbearable; again and again, you did not rush me, dismiss me, or let me disappear inside my grief.

You listened without judgment.
You challenged me without breaking me.
You reminded me of who I was when I was in danger of forgetting.

In moments when I wanted to stop existing altogether, you helped me stay. In seasons when I could not see purpose beyond the pain, you helped me find meaning without minimizing what I had lost.

This book is rooted in countless conversations, some heavy, some healing, some filled with laughter in the middle of tears. It exists because you held space for my pain while quietly insisting on my growth.

You helped me survive long enough to understand.
You helped me become brave enough to speak.

This book is yours as much as mine.

With all my love and gratitude,
*Venus*

# VENUS CHANDLER

# TABLE OF CONTENTS

# AUTHOR'S NOTE

I did not write this book as a reaction.
I wrote it as a response; born out of lived experience, reflection, and hard-earned understanding.

Since 2016, over the course of nearly a decade, I have lived the quiet reality of parental estrangement. A few years after that time, I became estranged from my son. I was also estranged from my daughter, reconnected, and then found myself estranged again. For a long time, I could not understand why this was happening. I searched myself endlessly, replayed conversations, questioned every decision, and carried a weight that few people openly talk about.

Before I had language, context, or understanding, the pain felt unbearable. There were moments when the grief was so heavy that I wanted to check out entirely; to disappear, to stop existing. The ache of being cut off from your own children defies logic and explanation. It is a kind of loss that has no funeral, no closure, and no public permission to grieve.

But over time, I chose education over despair.

Through study, observation, conversations, and deep self-examination, I began to understand that what I was experiencing was not isolated, rare, or uniquely personal. It was part of a much larger cultural shift; one that is now affecting families across generations, communities, and countries. Parental estrangement, particularly in the absence of abuse, addiction, or danger, has become a growing and largely unspoken global phenomenon.

7

# VENUS CHANDLER

I believe deeply in boundaries. I teach them. I live them. I have watched boundaries save lives, protect dignity, and restore self-worth. But I have also witnessed boundary language being misused, transformed into ultimatums, control mechanisms, and tools for avoiding accountability rather than fostering growth.

This book is not written to shame children or absolve parents. It is written to ask the questions many are afraid to voice. What happens when discomfort is labeled harm? When disagreement is rebranded as toxicity? When "protecting my peace" becomes justification for permanent disconnection rather than a pause for repair?

Families are not meant to be places of perpetual comfort. They are meant to be places of development. Growth requires tension. Maturity requires accountability. Love requires endurance.

I am writing this book not from bitterness, but from clarity. Not from blame, but from understanding. I now see with greater precision why this is happening, and why so many parents are silently carrying the same confusion, grief, and unanswered questions I once carried.

This book is an invitation; not to tolerate harm, but to reconsider distance as a default response. It is a call back to discernment, emotional maturity, and the belief that accountability and compassion can coexist.

We cannot heal what we refuse to examine.
We cannot restore what we are unwilling to confront.

This book is my contribution to that examination.

— *Venus Chandler*

# FOREWORD

Some books are written because the author has something to say. Others are written because silence has become too costly.

*Cut Off: Boundaries, Entitlement, and the Breakdown of Family Accountability* was not born from theory or trend. It was born from lived endurance, the kind that reshapes a person slowly, privately, and irrevocably.

I have watched Venus Chandler walk through one of the most isolating experiences a parent can endure: being estranged from her children. Not once, but repeatedly. I have watched her sit with questions that have no easy answers and carry grief that offers no public permission to mourn. I have watched her choose reflection over resentment and understanding over collapse.

This book exists because she refused to let pain have the final word.

What makes this work both timely and necessary is Venus's refusal to simplify what is complex. She does not deny the reality of harm where harm exists. She does not dismiss the importance of boundaries or personal agency.

Instead, she asks the questions many are afraid to ask: What happens when boundaries are used to avoid accountability? When discomfort is mistaken for danger? When distance replaces dialogue before repair has even been attempted?

These pages give language to a growing, global experience that has largely been suffered in silence. They offer clarity without cruelty and challenge without condemnation. This is not a book that demands agreement, it invites discernment.

I have seen Venus transform private grief into public contribution. I have watched her do the slow work of understanding, not to reclaim control, but to reclaim truth. This manuscript is the result of that work.

It is not written in anger.
It is written in wisdom.

And for many families, it will feel like the first honest conversation they have been allowed to have.

*Audrea V. Abraham*
Author & CEO Of IBG Publications, Inc.

# CHAPTER 1:

## When Distance Became The Default

There was a time when cutting off a parent was unthinkable except in the most extreme circumstances. Estrangement was rare, deliberate, and painful, an act of last resort when safety, stability, or sobriety could not be maintained. It was not casual. It was not encouraged, and it was certainly not celebrated.

Today, that has changed.

Across cultures, socioeconomic classes, and belief systems, an increasing number of adult children are choosing no contact with their parents. This shift has occurred rapidly, quietly, and with very little public scrutiny. What was once framed as a measure of protection is now often framed as empowerment. Distance is described as strength. Silence is described as healing. Removal is described as self-care.

The question is not whether no contact is ever necessary. In some cases, it absolutely is. The more pressing question is why it has become the *default* response to conflict, disappointment, and unmet expectations, even in the absence of abuse, addiction, or danger.

## *From Last Resort To First Response*

Historically, family estrangement carried social weight. It was met with concern, intervention, and often an assumption that something had gone deeply wrong. Extended family members asked questions. Communities noticed absences. Reconciliation, when possible, was encouraged.

In contrast, modern estrangement is frequently met with applause. Social media reinforces it. Popular psychology soundbites justify it. Entire online communities exist to validate cutting people off without context, nuance, or examination.

What was once a difficult decision now comes pre-packaged with language that removes discomfort from the choice itself. Phrases like *"I'm protecting my peace," "I don't owe anyone access to me,"* and *"Boundaries don't require explanation"* have become cultural shields; statements that shut down dialogue rather than invite understanding.

Distance has become normalized, and idealized.

## *The Redefinition Of Boundaries*

Boundaries are not new. They are a foundational component of healthy relationships. At their core, boundaries are about self-regulation; what I will accept, what I will tolerate, and how I will respond when those limits are crossed.

What boundaries are not meant to be is a tool for controlling others.

Yet increasingly, boundaries are being defined not as internal commitments but as external demands. They sound less like *"I will remove myself if this continues"* and more like *"You must behave in a way that meets my expectations, or I will remove you."*

# CUT OFF

This shift is subtle but significant. It moves the responsibility away from personal regulation and places it squarely on the other person's compliance. When parents do not comply, when they say no, disagree, or fail to align perfectly with their adult child's worldview, distance becomes the consequence.

This is not boundary-setting. It is a *'conditional relationship.'*

## *Discomfort Is Not Harm*

One of the most consequential cultural shifts contributing to estrangement is the reclassification of discomfort as danger. In a society increasingly intolerant of emotional distress, disagreement is often experienced as invalidation, and frustration is interpreted as threat.

Parents, by nature of their role, are often the first to say no. They are the first to challenge thinking, to question decisions, to offer perspective that may not feel affirming in the moment. This is not cruelty, it is guidance. It is how emotional resilience and discernment are developed.

When discomfort is pathologized, however, these ordinary relational tensions are rebranded as toxic. A parent who expresses concern becomes controlling. A boundary from a parent becomes disrespect. A refusal to comply becomes emotional harm.

In this environment, walking away feels justified, even necessary.

### *The Loss Of Relational Endurance*

Healthy relationships require endurance. They require the ability to remain present through misunderstanding, to repair after rupture, and to tolerate emotional discomfort without severing connection.

Many adult children today were never taught how to do this.

To be emotionally supportive, many parents avoided conflict, minimized consequences, and prioritized their children's comfort over resilience. While well-intentioned, this approach often left children ill-equipped to manage relational tension in adulthood.

When relationships become difficult, the instinct is not to engage, it is to exit.

Estrangement, in this context, becomes less about safety and more about skill deficit. The absence of tools for repair makes removal feel like the only option.

## *Silence As A Form of Power*

There is also an unspoken dynamic at play: silence confers power. When one party cuts off communication entirely, they control the narrative, the access, and the outcome. Parents are left without information, explanation, or recourse.

This dynamic is rarely discussed openly, yet it is deeply influential. Silence prevents accountability. It removes the possibility of mutual understanding. It freezes the relationship at the moment of conflict, allowing no room for growth, perspective, or change.

What is lost in the process is not just the relationship itself, but the opportunity for maturity on both sides.

## *A Question Worth Asking*

If no contact is truly about healing, why does it so often leave unresolved grief, anger, and identity fractures in its wake? Why do so many estranged families remain stuck, unable to move forward, yet unable to reconnect?

These questions are not accusations. They are invitations.

# CUT OFF

Before we can understand the full cost of estrangement, we must first understand how distance became easier than dialogue, and why cutting off began to feel safer than staying in the room.

This is where the conversation begins.

*"Distance was never meant to be the default; it became the norm when dialogue felt too costly and discomfort was rebranded as harm."*

-Coach Venus

# CHAPTER 2:

## Boundaries Aren't Ultimatums

Few concepts have gained as much cultural authority in recent years as boundaries. The word itself now carries moral weight. To say "this is my boundary" is often treated as unquestionable, final, and beyond examination. Yet the elevation of boundaries without a shared understanding of what they are has created confusion and, in many families, quiet devastation.

Boundaries are essential. Ultimatums are corrosive.
The tragedy is that the two are now frequently confused.

### *What Boundaries Were Always Meant To Be*

At their core, boundaries are internal commitments. They define how an individual will respond to behavior, not how others must behave to maintain relationships.

#### *A boundary sounds like:*

- *"If this conversation becomes disrespectful, I will step away."*

- *"I will not engage in discussions that escalate into personal attacks."*

- *"I need space right now, and I will reach out when I am ready to talk."*

Each of these statements centers responsibility where it belongs, on the individual setting the boundary. There is clarity without coercion. Choice without threat.

Healthy boundaries preserve dignity on both sides.

## *When Boundaries Become Conditions*

An ultimatum, by contrast, is externally focused. It demands compliance as the price of relationship. It sounds like:

- *"If you don't agree with me, I'm done."*

- *"You must change your beliefs, or you won't have access to me."*

- *"If you don't apologize the way I want, we're finished."*

These statements are not about protection. They are about control.

When boundaries are framed as conditions for access rather than guidelines for engagement, they cease to be tools for health and become instruments of leverage. The relationship is no longer mutual; it is transactional.

In parent-child dynamics, particularly when children reach adulthood, this shift is especially destabilizing. Parents are expected to comply indefinitely, regardless of their own values, boundaries, or lived wisdom, or risk permanent disconnection.

# CUT OFF

## *Authority Rebranded As Harm*

One of the most damaging narratives fueling estrangement is the idea that parental authority itself is inherently oppressive. In this framework, any expression of guidance, concern, or disagreement is interpreted as control.

A parent who says, *"I don't agree with that choice,"* is not necessarily attempting to dominate. They may be offering perspective shaped by experience. A parent who says no is not automatically invalidating autonomy. They may be exercising discernment.

Yet in a culture that prioritizes emotional affirmation above all else, authority is easily reframed as threat. When affirmation becomes the standard for love, disagreement becomes disqualifying.

The result is a fragile relational structure; one that cannot tolerate difference.

## *Emotional Safety vs. Emotional Comfort*

A crucial distinction is often overlooked: emotional safety is not the same as emotional comfort.

Emotional safety means one is not demeaned, threatened, or violated. Emotional comfort means one is not challenged, frustrated, or disappointed. Families are meant to provide safety, but they are not meant to eliminate discomfort entirely.

Growth requires friction. Perspective requires challenge. Maturity requires the ability to remain regulated in the presence of differing views.

When emotional comfort is elevated to a non-negotiable requirement, boundaries become shields against growth rather than support for health.

## *The Language That Ends Conversations*

Modern boundary language often shuts down dialogue instead of clarifying it. Statements like *"I don't owe you an explanation"* may feel empowering, but they also foreclose the possibility of understanding.

In healthy relationships, especially familial ones, explanation is not entitlement. It is an act of respect. Silence may protect the individual in the short term, but it impoverishes the relationship long term.

Cutting off communication without context freezes both parties in confusion. Parents are left to guess what went wrong. Adult children are left without the opportunity to practice articulation, repair, or reconciliation.

Boundaries should create clarity, not erase it.

## *The Cost Of Conditional Connection*

When connection becomes conditional upon agreement, relationships become unstable. Any divergence: political, spiritual, relational, or personal, threatens the bond.

This dynamic trains adult children to associate disagreement with abandonment and parents to associate honesty with loss. Over time, both sides learn to self-censor or disengage entirely.

What is lost is authenticity. What replaces it is fear. Families cannot thrive under the constant threat of erasure.

## *A More Responsible Use Of Boundaries*

Responsible boundaries invite conversation. They allow for pauses without permanence. They make room for difference without demanding sameness.

# CUT OFF

***They sound like:***

- *"I need space right now, but I'm open to talking later."*

- *"We see this differently, and that's hard for me, but I don't want to lose the relationship."*

- *"I'm setting limits, not closing the door."*

These boundaries protect without punishing. They honor autonomy without dissolving accountability.

## *The Question Beneath The Boundary*

When no contact is framed as a boundary, an important question must be asked: Is this decision protecting safety, or avoiding discomfort?

This question is not meant to shame. It is meant to clarify. Because the long-term consequences of estrangement are profound, and decisions made in moments of emotional intensity often outlast the circumstances that created them.

Boundaries are meant to help relationships survive difficulty, not justify their disappearance.

In the next chapter, we will examine the cultural environment that made ultimatums feel necessary, and why an entire generation has become increasingly intolerant of emotional discomfort.

*"A boundary sets a line for self-respect. An ultimatum builds a wall for control. Know the difference before you sever connection in the name of healing."*

**-Coach Venus**

# CHAPTER 3:

## A Culture Allergic To Discomfort

Discomfort was once understood as a natural part of growth. It signaled learning, stretching, and maturation. Today, discomfort is increasingly treated as something to be eliminated, avoided at all costs and interpreted as evidence that something is wrong.

This shift has quietly reshaped how relationships function, especially within families.

We are living in a culture that does not teach people how to endure emotional tension. Instead, it teaches them how to escape it.

### *When Feelings Became Final*

Emotions are important. They provide information, signal needs, and reflect internal states. But emotions were never meant to be the final authority in decision-making. They are data, not verdicts.

In today's climate, however, feelings are often elevated to indisputable truth. If something feels uncomfortable, it is assumed to be harmful. If a relationship produces distress, it is assumed to be unhealthy. If a conversation creates emotional tension, it is assumed to be unsafe.

This framework leaves little room for nuance. It eliminates the possibility that discomfort might be instructive rather than injurious.

Families, by their nature, surface unresolved beliefs, generational differences, and emotional blind spots. They are one of the few environments where people are not curated to our preferences. When discomfort becomes unacceptable, family relationships become especially vulnerable.

## *The Decline Of Distress Tolerance*

Distress tolerance is the ability to remain emotionally regulated in the presence of frustration, disappointment, or disagreement. This is a learned skill, developed over time through exposure, guidance, and repair.

Many adults today were never taught this skill.

To be emotionally supportive, many caregivers shielded children from frustration, stepped in too quickly to resolve conflict, and minimized discomfort whenever possible. While well-intentioned, this approach often prevented children from learning how to self-soothe, articulate disagreement, or stay engaged when emotions run high. As a result, emotional distress now feels intolerable rather than manageable.

When these individuals encounter relational tension in adulthood, especially with parents, the instinct is not to navigate through it. It is to remove it.

## *Avoidance Disguised As Self-Care*

Self-care is essential. Rest, boundaries, and emotional awareness are critical to well-being. But self-care has increasingly been redefined as avoidance.

Avoiding difficult conversations is framed as protecting peace. Cutting people off is framed as choosing oneself. Refusing engagement is framed as strength. What is rarely discussed is what avoidance costs.

Avoidance may reduce anxiety in the short term, but it often intensifies it over time. Unspoken grievances do not disappear; they harden. Unresolved conflict does not heal; it lingers. Distance does not automatically create peace, it often creates ambiguity, resentment, and unresolved grief. True self-care includes the ability to tolerate discomfort long enough to seek understanding.

## *The Echo Chamber Effect*

Another contributing factor is the rise of echo chambers; spaces where beliefs are continuously reinforced without challenge. Social media algorithms reward agreement and penalize dissent. Content that affirms personal narratives spreads faster than content that invites reflection.

In these environments, cutting people off is rarely questioned. In fact, it is often encouraged. Entire communities exist to validate estrangement without context, investigation, or accountability.

When individuals are surrounded exclusively by voices that affirm their choices, self-examination becomes unnecessary. Discomfort is no longer something to be worked through; it is something to be escaped. Families who naturally disrupt echo chambers become casualties of this dynamic.

## *Conflict Reframed As Incompatibility*

Disagreement used to be understood as a normal part of relationship. Today, it is often reframed as incompatibility.

If values differ, the relationship is deemed unworkable. If perspectives clash, the bond is labeled unhealthy. If growth requires negotiation, the relationship is judged as too costly.

This binary thinking leaves no space for complexity. Relationships are either affirming or disposable. People are either supportive or toxic. There is no middle ground for imperfection, misunderstanding, or gradual change.

Families, which require patience and endurance, cannot survive under such rigid expectations.

## *The Illusion Of Control*

Discomfort also threatens the illusion of control. Staying in difficult relationships requires humility, the acknowledgment that we cannot fully control others' beliefs, reactions, or growth timelines.

Cutting off provides immediate control. It removes uncertainty. It ends the tension.

But control is not the same as resolution.

When control replaces communication, growth stalls. The individual may feel empowered, but the underlying relational skills remain undeveloped.

## *What Is Lost When Discomfort Is Avoided*

Avoiding discomfort may feel protective, but it often costs individuals the opportunity to develop:

- Emotional resilience

- Conflict resolution skills

- Perspective-taking

- Relational endurance

- Identity grounded in more than emotional reactivity

Families are one of the primary environments where these capacities are meant to be formed and refined. When family relationships are abandoned at the first sign of sustained discomfort, these skills remain underdeveloped.

The cost is not only relational, but also developmental.

## *A Necessary Reframe*

Discomfort is not the enemy. It is information. It signals where growth is needed, where expectations must be examined, and where communication skills must be strengthened.

The goal is not to remain in harmful situations. The goal is to learn how to discern harm from discomfort, and how to respond to each appropriately. When a culture teaches people to flee discomfort rather than understand it, estrangement becomes inevitable.

In the next section of this book, we will examine how entitlement, often disguised as empowerment, has further destabilized family relationships and contributed to the expectation that parents must comply indefinitely or lose access altogether.

*"We were never meant to run from discomfort; we were meant to grow through it. Maturity lives on the other side of uncomfortable conversations."*

-Coach Venus

# CHAPTER 4:

## The Expectation Of Parental Compliance

One of the least discussed dynamics behind modern estrangement is not cruelty, neglect, or abandonment, but expectation. Specifically, the expectation that parents must continue to comply emotionally, financially, ideologically, and relationally with their adult children to maintain access.

This expectation is rarely stated outright. Instead, it is implied, enforced indirectly, and justified through the language of boundaries and self-care. When parents do not meet these expectations, distance becomes the consequence.

Estrangement, in this context, is not about safety. It is about leverage.

### *When Adulthood Still Requires Permission From Parents*

Adulthood is meant to mark a shift toward independence, responsibility, and mutual respect. Adult children gain autonomy over their lives, choices, and identities. Parents, in turn, shift from authority figures to advisors, offering perspective without control. Instead, what has emerged in many families is a reversal of responsibility.

Parents are expected to adapt indefinitely. Their role becomes one of affirmation without input, support without opinion, and presence without perspective. Any deviation, any disagreement, hesitation, or refusal, is framed as invalidation. In this model, parents are not allowed to remain whole individuals. They must contort themselves to preserve access.

## *Agreement As The Price Of Relationship*

The most destabilizing aspect of this expectation is that agreement becomes the currency of connection.

### *Parents are expected to:*

- Affirm decisions they may genuinely believe are harmful.

- Apologize for boundaries they have a right to set.

- Accept rewritten narratives without response.

- Remain silent to avoid conflict.

- Fund choices they do not support.

- Validate feelings while being denied their own.

When parents decline to do so, they are often accused of being unsupportive, controlling, or emotionally unsafe. This dynamic teaches adult children that disagreement equals rejection and teaches parents that honesty risks erasure.

*Neither outcome fosters healthy relationships.*

# CUT OFF

## *The Fear Of Losing Access*

Many parents comply not because they agree, but because they are afraid. Afraid that one wrong word will result in silence. Afraid that boundaries of their own will be punished. Afraid that asserting themselves will cost them their children entirely. This fear is powerful and it is rarely acknowledged.

Parents begin to self-censor, second-guess, and over-apologize. They shrink themselves emotionally in the hope of maintaining connection. Over time, resentment grows quietly beneath the surface, even as access is preserved. This is not peace. It is emotional hostage-taking, though it is rarely named as such.

## *Entitlement Without Reciprocity*

Healthy adult relationships are reciprocal. Both parties are allowed boundaries. Both parties are allowed disagreement. Both parties are allowed growth. Entitlement emerges when one party believes their needs, emotions, and expectations outweigh the other's indefinitely.

In many estranged families, adult children claim the right to full autonomy while denying parents the right to perspective. They demand respect without offering it. They insist on validation without dialogue.

Accountability becomes optional, reserved for the parent, never the child.

## *When Boundaries Replace Maturity*

Boundaries are often used as substitutes for emotional maturity. Instead of learning how to negotiate differences, articulate needs clearly, or tolerate frustration, individuals default to withdrawal. Compliance becomes an unspoken requirement for connection. When it is not met, the relationship is deemed unsafe.

This dynamic removes the incentive to grow relational skills. Why learn how to communicate when silence is easier? Why risk vulnerability when control is more efficient?

*But efficiency is not intimacy.*

## *Parents As Scapegoats For Discomfort*

Another consequence of this expectation is that parents become repositories for unresolved frustration. When adult life becomes difficult, as it inevitably does, parents are often blamed for emotional discomfort that originates elsewhere.

Rather than confronting external challenges, some adult children redirect dissatisfaction toward their parents. Estrangement offers a sense of relief, a clear villain, and a simplified narrative.

The complexity of adulthood is reduced to a relational rupture that feels decisive, even empowering.

## *The Long-Term Cost Of Compliance*

While compliance may preserve access in the short term, it comes at a cost. Parents lose their voice. Relationships lose authenticity. Children lose the opportunity to engage with differing perspectives safely. Over time, the relationship becomes hollow, maintained through silence rather than connection.

When compliance eventually fails, as it often does, estrangement arrives anyway, leaving parents exhausted and confused, wondering where the line was crossed.

## *A Necessary Question*

*At the heart of this dynamic lies a critical question:*

Is the relationship being preserved through mutual respect, or enforced through fear of loss? Until this question is examined honestly, estrangement will continue to be framed as empowerment rather than what it often is: an avoidance of the hard work required for adult relationships to mature.

In the next chapter, we will explore how emotional absolutism, the belief that feelings alone determine truth, has further dismantled accountability and made estrangement feel morally justified.

*"Parents were not created to mirror your every belief; they were created to raise you with wisdom. Honor doesn't require agreement, just maturity."*

-Coach Venus

# CHAPTER 5:

## "My Feelings Are Final"

*Feelings matter.*

They signal internal experiences, unmet needs, and emotional responses to the world around us. But feelings were never meant to function as final authority. They are meant to be examined, not obeyed unquestioningly.

Yet in many modern family dynamics, feelings have become decisive rather than informative. How someone feels is treated as sufficient justification for permanent decisions, without reflection, dialogue, or responsibility for interpretation. This shift has profound consequences.

## *When Feelings Become Facts*

Emotional absolutism is the belief that feelings are inherently factual, self-validating, and beyond challenge. If something feels wrong, it is wrong. If someone feels hurt, someone else must be at fault. If discomfort arises, removal is justified. This framework collapses the distinction between experience and interpretation.

A parent's comment may feel dismissive, but was it intended that way? A disagreement may feel invalidating, but does it constitute harm? Emotional absolutism removes the need to ask these questions. Feelings become evidence. Context becomes irrelevant.

When feelings are treated as facts, accountability dissolves.

## *The Elimination Of Self-Reflection*

Healthy emotional development requires self-reflection, the ability to examine one's own reactions, triggers, expectations, and assumptions. Emotional absolutism discourages this process.

***Instead of asking:***

- *Why did this affect me so strongly?*

- *What expectation did I bring into this interaction?*

- *Is my reaction proportional to the situation?*

***The focus shifts outward:***

- *They made me feel this way.*

- *They are the problem.*

- *They need to change.*

This externalization of responsibility makes growth impossible. Estrangement becomes a solution not because it resolves conflict, but because it removes the need for introspection.

## *Parents As Emotional Mirrors*

Parents often become emotional mirrors for their adult children; reflecting back beliefs, values, and behaviors that may be uncomfortable to confront. When parents do not affirm every feeling without question, they are perceived as invalidating. But emotional validation does not require emotional agreement.

A parent can acknowledge feelings without endorsing conclusions. They can say, *"I hear that you're hurt,"* without saying, *"I accept that I caused harm."*

When these distinctions are lost, parents are forced into impossible positions: either affirm interpretations they do not believe are accurate or risk losing access altogether.

### The Fragility Of Unchallenged Emotion

Unexamined emotions are fragile. When feelings are never questioned, tested, or contextualized, they harden into identity. Any challenge feels like an attack. Any disagreement feels like erasure.

This fragility makes relationships unstable. There is no room for misunderstanding, growth, or repair, only affirmation or abandonment. Families, which require tolerance for emotional complexity, cannot survive under these conditions.

### Estrangement As Emotional Certainty

Estrangement provides emotional certainty. It offers a clean narrative: *I am right. They are wrong. Distance proves my strength.*

Estrangement often freezes emotions at the moment of conflict. There is no opportunity for perspective to mature, for emotions to soften, or for understanding to evolve. What feels empowering in the short term can become limiting over time.

### The Absence Of Emotional Responsibility

Emotional responsibility means recognizing that feelings, while valid, are not self-explanatory. They require interpretation, regulation, and communication.

*In emotionally responsible relationships:*

- Feelings are expressed without accusation

- Interpretations are offered with humility

- Accountability is shared rather than assigned

Emotional absolutism rejects this framework. It positions feelings as untouchable and exempts the individual from responsibility for how those feelings are acted upon. Silence becomes justified. Distance becomes moral. Dialogue becomes unnecessary.

## *The Cost To Parents*

For parents, emotional absolutism creates a no-win scenario. They are expected to accept emotional judgments without context or conversation. Attempts to clarify are labeled defensive. Requests for dialogue are labeled boundary violations.

Parents are left grieving not only the loss of relationships, but the loss of reality-sharing. They grieve the ability to speak openly, reflect together, and grow mutually. They are rendered voiceless in relationships they once carried.

## *A More Mature Emotional Framework*

Mature emotional engagement does not dismiss feelings, but it does not deny them either. It recognizes that feelings are signals, not sentences. They invite curiosity, not conclusions.

*It asks:*

- *What else might be true?*

- *What role did I play in this dynamic?*

- *What conversation is still needed?*

Without this framework, estrangement becomes inevitable—because any relationship that requires emotional complexity will eventually feel intolerable.

## *A Question Worth Sitting With*

Before severing a relationship based solely on emotion, a question must be asked: Am I responding to harm, or reacting to discomfort that I have not yet learned how to process?

The answer to that question often determines whether distance leads to healing or merely postpones growth.

In the next chapter, we will examine how therapeutic language, meant to support healing, has been repurposed in ways that shut down accountability and make estrangement socially unquestionable.

*"Feelings are valid, but not infallible. They require discernment, not domination. Truth must be tested, not just felt."*

-Coach Venus

# CHAPTER 6:

## The Misuse Of Therapeutic Language

***Language shapes perception.***

It determines what we question, what we excuse, and what we condemn. Few language systems carry as much authority today as therapeutic language, terms originally developed to describe clinical harm, trauma, and psychological injury.

When used accurately, this language is lifesaving. When misused, it becomes silencing.

In modern family estrangement, therapeutic language has increasingly been detached from its clinical meaning and repurposed as moral judgment. Words once reserved for abuse and pathology are now applied to ordinary relational conflict, disagreement, and emotional discomfort.

The result is a conversation that cannot be challenged; questioning the language appears unsafe.

### *From Clinical Terms To Cultural Weapons*

Words like *toxic, unsafe, narcissistic, emotionally abusive,* and *triggering* once described specific patterns of behavior requiring professional discernment. Today, they are often applied broadly, without context, evidence, or differentiation.

A parent who disagrees becomes *toxic.*
A boundary set by a parent becomes *control.*
A difficult conversation becomes *emotional harm.*
A refusal to comply becomes *narcissism.*

These labels carry heavy implications. Once applied, they end dialogue. They transform complex relationships into one-dimensional narratives of victims and villains. Therapeutic language, in this form, no longer facilitates healing, it forecloses it.

## *Labeling As A Substitute For Conversation*

Labels are efficient. They reduce complexity and eliminate the need for explanation. If someone is labeled unsafe, no further engagement is required. If someone is labeled toxic, distance is justified without discussion. But healing requires articulation. It requires naming behaviors, expressing impact, and allowing response. Labels skip these steps.

In families, this dynamic is particularly destructive. Parents are often assigned clinical labels without ever being told what specific behaviors caused harm, when they occurred, or what repair would look like.

*Silence replaces specificity. Diagnosis replaces dialogue.*

## *The Illusion Of Authority*

Therapeutic language carries the illusion of expertise. It sounds informed, professional, and morally grounded, even when it is used incorrectly.

This illusion creates an imbalance of power. The person using the language positions themselves as emotionally enlightened, while the other party is cast as deficient or dangerous. Any attempt to question the narrative is dismissed as denial or manipulation.

Parents, already navigating generational differences in language and

culture, are especially vulnerable to this dynamic. They are often unfamiliar with terminology but acutely aware of its consequences.

## *When Healing Language Discourages Accountability*

Ironically, the misuse of therapeutic language often undermines the very accountability therapy is meant to foster.

***True therapeutic work emphasizes:***

- Self-reflection

- Personal responsibility

- Pattern recognition

- Emotional regulation

- Repair and integration

Weaponized therapeutic language does the opposite. It externalizes blame, solidifies identity around injury, and removes the need for reciprocal accountability.

Estrangement becomes framed not as a choice, but as a diagnosis-driven necessity, beyond question or reconsideration.

## *Parents As Unlicensed Diagnoses*

Many parents report being diagnosed, informally, unilaterally, and without recourse by their own children. Labels are delivered without conversation, assessment, or opportunity for response.

*These diagnoses often come without:*

- Specific examples

- Clear expectations for change

- Timeframes for repair

- Willingness to engage

Instead, the label itself becomes the justification for permanent distance. This is not therapeutic practice. It is relational foreclosure.

## The Chilling Effect On Repair

Once therapeutic language is weaponized, repair becomes nearly impossible. Parents are afraid to speak for fear of reinforcing the label. Apologies are dismissed as manipulative. Growth is not acknowledged because the narrative requires stagnation. The relationship freezes in a moment of accusation, with no mechanism for movement. Healing language, when misused, does not open doors. It seals them shut.

## Therapy Was Never Meant To Erase Relationship

Therapy was designed to help people understand themselves better, not to absolve them of relational responsibility. It was meant to improve communication, not eliminate it. It was meant to foster insight, not superiority.

When therapy language is used to justify permanent disconnection without dialogue, it has drifted far from its original purpose. This is not an indictment of therapy. It is a call for discernment in how therapeutic concepts are applied, especially within families where long-term relational consequences are at stake.

## *A Necessary Distinction*

There is a critical difference between identifying harmful behavior and labeling a person as irredeemable. Between naming impact and assigning pathology. Between protecting oneself and punishing another. Without this distinction, estrangement becomes socially unquestionable and emotionally irreversible.

## *The Question Beneath The Language*

Before cutting off a parent using therapeutic labels, an essential question must be asked: Have I described specific behaviors and invited accountability, or have I used language to avoid conversation altogether?

The answer to that question often reveals whether healing is the goal, or whether certainty has replaced curiosity.

In the next chapter, we will turn toward the often-overlooked consequences of estrangement itself. We will evaluate what is lost (not only for parents) but for children who cut off connections in the absence of true harm.

*"Healing language was never meant to be a weapon. When we label what we refuse to confront, we shut the door on restoration."*

-Coach Venus

# CHAPTER 7:

## What Children Lose When They Cut Off

Estrangement is often discussed almost exclusively in terms of relief, relief from conflict, tension, or emotional discomfort. What is rarely discussed is what is lost when connection is severed, particularly in cases where no abuse, addiction, or danger is present.

Loss does not always announce itself immediately. In many cases, it unfolds quietly, over years.

### *The Loss Of Context*

*Parents hold context.*

They remember who you were before the story hardened, before the narrative solidified around a single season, decision, or conflict. They remember your beginnings, your temperament, your resilience, and your capacity long before adulthood complicated identity.

When parents are cut off, that living history is lost.

47

Without context, identity becomes narrower. Life is interpreted without the long view. Stories go unchallenged, and perspectives that once provided grounding disappear.

*This loss is subtle, but profound.*

## *The Loss Of Relational Skill-Building*

Family relationships are among the few that do not rely on compatibility alone. They require endurance, repair, and negotiation across differences. These skills are transferable. They shape how individuals handle friendships, partnerships, workplaces, and communities.

When adult children remove themselves from family relationships at the first sign of sustained discomfort, they lose one of the most formative environments for developing relational maturity. Walking away becomes the default problem-solving strategy. Over time, this pattern often repeats across relationships that begin to feel equally "unsafe" when conflict arises.

## *The Loss Of Being Known Beyond Agreement*

Parents often know their children in ways few others do; not because they are perfect observers, but because they have seen the full arc of growth, failure, resilience, and change. When relationships are contingent upon agreement, this kind of knowing disappears.

Adult children may find themselves surrounded by people who affirm them, but who cannot challenge them without risking removal. Affirmation replaces depth. Agreement replaces intimacy. What is lost is the experience of being known and loved in difference.

# CUT OFF

## *The Loss Of Legacy And Continuity*

Families carry legacy, stories, values, lessons learned the hard way. Even when those legacies are imperfect, they provide continuity and grounding. Cutting off parents often severs access to this inheritance, not just materially, but emotionally and historically.

This loss becomes more apparent with time: during major life transitions, aging, illness, and moments when perspective is needed rather than validation. Legacy is not always comfortable, but it is formative.

## *The Loss Of Reconciliation Skills*

Reconciliation is not the same as reconciliation *without accountability*. It is the process of naming harm, expressing impact, taking responsibility, and choosing repair.

When estrangement is chosen instead of reconciliation, the skill of repair remains underdeveloped. Future conflicts are handled through distance rather than dialogue. This can create a cycle where relationships are repeatedly abandoned rather than matured.

## *The Loss Of Future Repair*

Estrangement often feels permanent in the moment, but life is not static. People change. Perspectives soften. Understanding deepens.

When contact is severed without openness to future repair, the opportunity for mutual growth disappears. Parents age. Circumstances shift. Questions go unanswered.

The door that was closed for protection becomes a door that cannot be reopened without regret.

## *The Emotional Debt That Remains*

Avoidance does not eliminate emotional debt, it defers it.

Many adult children who cut off parents report that unresolved emotions resurface later in life: during parenting, grief, illness, or moments of vulnerability. Without access to the original relationship, these emotions have nowhere to go.

The cost of avoidance often appears long after the relief has faded.

## *A Necessary Distinction*

Not all estrangement is wrong. Some distance is necessary. Some relationships cannot be safely repaired. But when estrangement is chosen primarily to avoid discomfort, disagreement, or accountability, the losses compound quietly and persistently.

The question is not whether cutting off brings relief. It often does. The question is whether it builds the capacity for the life and relationships one hopes to sustain long-term.

## *A Question Worth Asking*

Before severing a parental relationship permanently, it is worth asking: What am I protecting myself from, and what might I be depriving myself of? The answer to that question deserves time, honesty, and humility.

In the next chapter, we will turn toward the other side of estrangement, the often-invisible grief carried by parents, and the silence that surrounds it.

# CHAPTER 8:

## The Silent Grief Of Parents

There is a particular kind of grief that has no ritual, no public language, and no socially acceptable expression. It is the grief of parents whose children are still alive but no longer present.

This grief does not arrive with condolences or casseroles. It is carried quietly, often in isolation, because there is no clear script for mourning someone who has chosen absence.

### *Loss Without Permission To Grieve*

When a child dies, society understands how to respond. When a marriage ends, there is acknowledgment. When a parent is cut off, there is often silence, or worse, suspicion.

Parents are expected to explain themselves. To justify the loss. To accept blame without defense. Their grief is frequently minimized or dismissed with phrases like *"There must be a reason,"* or *"Maybe it's for the best."*

***This response denies parents the dignity of grief.***

Estrangement is not a neutral event. It is a rupture that carries emotional, psychological, and identity-level consequences.

## *The Collapse Of Parental Identity*

*Parenthood does not end when a child becomes an adult.*

It evolves; but it does not disappear. When a child cuts off contact,

Parenthood does not end when a child becomes an adult. It evolves, but it does not disappear. When a child cuts off contact, parents often experience a collapse of identity.

*Questions surface relentlessly:*

- *Who am I if I am not allowed to be a parent?*

- *What did I miss?*

- *What was rewritten without my knowledge?*

Parents replay memories endlessly, searching for the moment everything went wrong. They examine decisions made decades earlier, often without context or compassion for who they were at the time. This kind of grief is not linear. It resurfaces in waves: holidays, birthdays, milestones, quiet moments when absence is loudest.

## *The Pain Of Not Knowing*

One of the most devastating aspects of estrangement is the absence of explanation. Many parents are cut off without clarity, specificity, or opportunity for response.

*They are left guessing:*

- Was it something I said?

- Something I didn't say?

- Something I don't understand?

This ambiguity prevents closure. Without language, grief cannot settle. It remains suspended, unresolved and ongoing. The human mind seeks coherence. Estrangement without explanation denies that coherence and prolongs suffering.

## *Shame & Self-Silencing*

Parents often carry profound shame around estrangement. They hesitate to speak openly for fear of judgment, misunderstanding, or further rejection. They learn quickly that sharing their story invites scrutiny. Their pain is interrogated rather than acknowledged. Over time, many stop speaking altogether.

*Silence becomes both shield and sentence.*

This self-silencing compounds grief. It isolates parents at the very moment connection is most needed.

## *The Double Bind*

Estranged parents are trapped in a double bind. If they reach out, they risk reinforcing the narrative that they are intrusive or disrespectful. If they remain silent, they risk being accused of indifference.

There is no correct move. Every action, or inaction, can be interpreted as proof of wrongdoing. This dynamic erodes confidence and creates paralysis. Parents become afraid to exist in relationships at all.

## *Love Without Access*

Perhaps the most unbearable aspect of estrangement is loving without access. Parents do not stop caring when contact ends.

Concern does not dissipate with silence. Love does not require permission; but expression does.

*Parents wonder:*

- Are they safe?

- Are they well?

- Do they know I still care?

There is no way to ask. No way to show up. No way to be present.

This is not detachment. It is containment of love with nowhere to go.

## *The Longing For Repair*

Contrary to common assumptions, most estranged parents do not seek control. They seek understanding. They want clarity, conversation, and the possibility, however small, of repair.

Many are willing to listen. To reflect. To change where change is warranted. What they cannot do is repair a relationship they are not allowed to speak into. Repair requires participation from both sides. Silence forecloses that possibility.

## *Grief That Ages With Time*

Estrangement grief does not fade neatly. It changes form. As parents age, questions about legacy, memory, and meaning intensify.

- ✓ Who will remember the early years?
- ✓ Who will carry the stories forward?
- ✓ Who will be there at the end?

These questions are rarely voiced, but they weigh heavily. The pain of estrangement is not only about what was lost, but about what may never be regained.

## *Naming The Unspoken*

This chapter exists to name what is often ignored: parental estrangement is not a neutral boundary choice. It is a relational loss with real human cost.

Acknowledging this does not negate the experiences of adult children. It does not deny harm where harm exists. It simply recognizes that grief does not belong to only one side. Families fracture in silence when grief is allowed to remain unspoken.

In the next chapter, we will examine the long-term consequences of unresolved distance, and why estrangement, when chosen without accountability or repair, often leaves both sides suspended rather than healed.

*"There is no funeral for the estranged. No eulogy for the living child who walked away. Just an ache parents carry in silence."*

-Coach Venus

# CHAPTER 9:

## The Longevity Of Unresolved Distance

*Distance has a way of feeling temporary, at first.*

Silence is often framed as a pause, a reset, or a necessary season. Many who initiate no contact believe they will eventually feel relief, clarity, or peace that confirms the decision was right.

What is less discussed is what happens when distance is allowed to age without resolution. Time does not automatically heal what was never addressed.

### *When Silence Becomes A New Normal*

In the early stages of estrangement, silence can feel purposeful. It offers immediate relief from tension and emotional overwhelm. But over time, silence stops being intentional and becomes habitual.

Days turn into months. Months turn into years.

The absence that once felt controlled begins to feel fixed. Without active efforts toward understanding or repair, distance hardens into a new normal; one that no longer feels shocking but still carries weight.

## *The Freezing of Narrative*

Unresolved distance freezes narratives in place. The story told at the moment of estrangement becomes the story that endures. There is no opportunity for clarification. No room for growth. No allowance for changing perspective.

Parents are remembered as they were perceived in a moment of conflict, not as they may have become with reflection, accountability, or time. Adult children are remembered as they were at the moment of departure, not as they might have matured through continued relationship.

*Both sides are denied evolution.*

## *Deferred Grief*

Estrangement often postpones grief rather than resolving it. The emotional cost is deferred, not eliminated.

*Grief resurfaces during:*

- Major life milestones

- Illness or loss

- Aging and reflection

- Parenting one's own children

These moments expose absence in ways that distance alone cannot mitigate. Without a path for repair, grief becomes chronic; recurring rather than processed.

# CUT OFF

## *The Myth Of Closure Without Conversation*

Closure is frequently cited as a reason for cutting off contact. Yet closure rarely occurs without dialogue. Understanding requires exchange. Healing requires articulation. Closure requires context.

In the absence of conversation, individuals often create their own explanations, which remain untested and unresolved. These internal narratives may provide temporary certainty, but they often fail to bring peace. What feels like closure is often simply the end of engagement, not the end of impact.

## *The Emotional Cost Of Permanence*

As time passes, the permanence of estrangement becomes harder to ignore. Decisions once framed as temporary begin to carry irreversible weight.

Parents age. Health changes. Opportunities for reconciliation narrow.

Adult children may feel pressure to justify the distance, not because it still feels right, but because reversing it would require humility, vulnerability, and acknowledgment that the original decision may have been incomplete.

*Pride can become a barrier to repair.*

## *Identity In The Absence Of Relationship*

Relationships shape identity. When a foundational relationship is removed, identity reorganizes around absence. Adult children may define themselves in opposition to their parents rather than in relation to them. Parents may struggle to integrate estrangement into their sense of self without internalizing blame.

In both cases, the unresolved relationship continues to exert influence, despite the silence. Distance does not mean disengagement. It means influence without interaction.

## *The Narrowing Of Perspective*

Without ongoing relationships, perspective narrows. Assumptions remain unchallenged. Narratives harden.

Continued contact, even imperfect contact, allows for recalibration over time. Distance does not. The longer estrangement persists, the more difficult it becomes to imagine alternative interpretations or paths forward.

## *When Time Is No Longer Neutral*

Time is often treated as a neutral factor in estrangement. In reality, time exerts pressure.

It magnifies regret.
It amplifies unanswered questions.
It reduces opportunities for repair.

What could have been addressed with conversation becomes harder to approach after years of silence. Time, without intention, works against reconciliation.

## *A Different Use Of Distance*

Distance can be constructive when it is purposeful, time-limited, and oriented toward repair. It allows for reflection, emotional regulation, and preparation for dialogue.

Distance becomes destructive when it is indefinite, unexamined, and treated as resolution. The difference lies not in the space itself, but in what the space is meant to accomplish.

# CUT OFF

## *A Question That Time Eventually Asks*

As estrangement ages, one question inevitably emerges: Has this distance helped me become more whole, or merely more certain?

Certainty is not the same as growth. Silence is not the same as peace.

In the final section of this book, we will shift toward restoration, examining how accountability, discernment, and emotional maturity can create pathways forward without denying real harm where it exists.

*"Time does not heal what is avoided. It only hardens what was never humbled through conversation, honesty, and mutual care."*

-Coach Venus

# CHAPTER 10:

## Repair Is A Skill

Repair is not instinctive. It is learned.

Most people assume that reconciliation happens naturally when emotions cool or time passes. In reality, repair requires specific skills, skills that many families were never taught and many cultures no longer value.

When repair is absent, distance becomes the default.

### *The Myth Of Automatic Healing*

Time alone does not heal relational rupture. Without intention, time often reinforces misunderstanding rather than resolving it.

People change over time, but relationships do not heal without engagement. Healing requires naming harm, acknowledging impact, taking responsibility where appropriate, and creating new patterns of interaction.

When these steps are skipped, estrangement fills the gap left by missing skills.

## *What Repair Actually Requires*

Repair is not an apology alone. It is a process that includes:

- Willingness to listen without defensiveness.

- Capacity to tolerate discomfort.

- Ability to distinguish intent from impact.

- Ownership of one's role without self-erasure.

- Openness to reciprocal accountability.

These capacities are not innate. They must be developed. Families that lack these skills often mistake withdrawal for resolution.

## *The Difference Between Accountability And Self-Abandonment*

Many parents believe that repair requires surrendering their dignity. They assume they must accept every accusation, rewrite their memory, or erase their boundaries to restore contact.

*This is not repair; it is self-abandonment.*

True accountability allows individuals to acknowledge impact without forfeiting truth. It allows parents to say, *"I hear how that affected you,"* without saying, *"I accept a version of events that I do not believe is accurate."*

Repair cannot occur if one party is required to disappear for the relationship to continue.

## *Why Repair Feels Threatening*

Repair threatens certainty. It requires humility, flexibility, and the willingness to discover that one's understanding may be incomplete.

For adult children, repair may require acknowledging that parents are more complex than the narrative allows. For parents, it may require acknowledging blind spots or unintentional harm. Both positions involve vulnerability. Estrangement avoids this vulnerability by freezing the story in place.

## *Staying In The Room*

Repair requires staying in the room: emotionally and relationally, even when discomfort arises.

This does not mean tolerating abuse or harm. It means remaining engaged long enough to understand what is happening beneath the conflict.

Staying allows misunderstandings to be clarified, assumptions to be tested, and emotions to settle into perspective. Leaving forecloses these possibilities.

## *The Skill Of Listening Without Defense*

Defensiveness is one of the greatest obstacles to repair. It shuts down listening and escalates conflict.

Learning to listen without defense does not mean agreeing with everything said. It means temporarily suspending the need to correct or justify to understand. This skill is particularly difficult in parent-child dynamics, where emotions are layered with history, identity, and expectation. Without this skill, conversations collapse quickly, and distance feels safer.

## *Repair Is Mutual*

Repair cannot be one-sided. It requires willingness from both parties to engage, reflect, and change where appropriate. When only one side is expected to do the work, resentment replaces healing.

Estrangement often emerges not because repair is impossible, but because it has been misrepresented as submission.

## *The Courage To Try Again*

Repair involves risk. Conversations may be awkward. Emotions may surface. Outcomes are uncertain. But the absence of repair carries its own risk, the risk of permanent distance, unresolved grief, and foreclosed growth. Choosing repair does not guarantee reconciliation. It does guarantee integrity.

## *Reframing Strength*

Strength is often defined as independence and self-protection. Strength also includes endurance, humility, and the capacity to remain engaged under pressure.

Repair requires a different kind of strength; one that does not seek to win, but to understand.

## *A Question For The Reader*

Before concluding that estrangement is the only option, it is worth asking: Do I lack safety, or do I lack the skills needed to repair what is broken?

The answer to that question determines whether distance becomes a boundary, or a barrier.

In the next chapter, we will examine how families can teach resilience rather than reinforce avoidance, and why learning to stay is as important as knowing when to step away.

# CHAPTER 11:

## Teaching Children How To Stay

One of the greatest disservices of modern culture is not that it teaches people how to leave, it is that it fails to teach them how to stay.

Staying does not mean tolerating harm.
Staying means remaining engaged long enough for growth, understanding, and repair to occur.

***This distinction has been largely lost.***

### *The Disappearance Of Relational Endurance*

Relational endurance is the capacity to remain present during discomfort without defaulting to withdrawal. It is the ability to tolerate frustration, disagreement, and emotional tension without interpreting them as threats.

This capacity must be taught. It does not develop automatically.

When children are raised in environments where discomfort is quickly removed, conflict is avoided, or emotions are treated as emergencies, they do not learn how to regulate themselves in relational tension. They learn that leaving is the safest option. As adults, this lesson follows them into their most important relationships.

## *Protection Without Preparation*

Many parents, motivated by love, attempted to protect their children from the emotional difficulties they themselves endured. They softened consequences, avoided confrontation, and prioritized comfort.

### *What was often missing was preparation.*

Protection without preparation leaves children vulnerable; not resilient. It teaches them how to avoid pain, but not how to endure it. It teaches them how to exit, but not how to engage. Families then pay the price later, when adult children lack the skills needed to remain in relationship through inevitable conflict.

## *Modeling Matters More Than Instruction*

Children learn how to handle relationships by watching how adults handle them.

### *They learn:*

- How disagreement is managed.

- How apologies are made.

- How repair is attempted.

- How emotions are regulated.

- How boundaries are expressed.

# CUT OFF

When parents model withdrawal, silence, or avoidance, children internalize those responses. When parents model engagement, reflection, and repair, children learn that conflict does not require disconnection. Teaching children how to stay begins with adults staying themselves.

## *Boundaries That Invite Relationship*

Healthy boundaries do not end relationships, they shape them.

Children who are taught that boundaries exist to preserve connection, rather than eliminate them, are more likely to use them responsibly. They learn that limits can coexist with love, and that distance does not have to mean disappearance.

This requires parents to articulate boundaries clearly and consistently, while remaining emotionally available.

Boundaries that invite relationship say:

- *"I need a pause, not an ending."*

- *"This matters enough to talk about."*

- *"I'm staying engaged, even when it's hard."*

## *Allowing Discomfort Without Rescue*

One of the most powerful ways to teach resilience is to allow discomfort without immediately rescuing. This does not mean ignoring pain or dismissing emotion. It means resisting the urge to fix everything instantly.

When children are allowed to sit with frustration, disappointment, or disagreement, and are supported rather than rescued, they learn that discomfort is survivable.

This lesson is foundational. Without it, adulthood becomes a series of exits.

## *Teaching Repair Explicitly*

Repair should be taught explicitly, not assumed.

*Children need to learn:*

- How to apologize meaningfully.

- How to name impact without accusation.

- How to listen without interrupting.

- How to express needs without ultimatums.

- How to return to relationship after rupture.

When repair is normalized, conflict loses its threat. Relationships become flexible rather than fragile.

## *The Difference Between Independence And Isolation*

Independence is the ability to stand on one's own while remaining connected. Isolation is standing alone because connection feels unsafe or overwhelming.

When staying is framed as weakness, isolation masquerades as strength. Teaching children how to stay means teaching them that independence does not require disconnection, and that autonomy does not require abandonment.

## *Preparing for Adult Relationships*

Family relationships are training grounds for adult relationships. The patterns learned at home often repeat elsewhere.

*Children who learn to stay:*

- Navigate workplace conflict more effectively.

- Maintain long-term parnerships.

- Engage in community without fragmentation.

- Handle difference without panic.

Children who learn to leave often struggle to sustain relationships that require negotiation, patience, and humility.

## *A Cultural Correction*

Teaching children how to stay is a corrective to a culture that rewards avoidance. It is a commitment to long-term relational health over short-term emotional relief. It does not deny harm. It does not minimize pain. It simply refuses to treat withdrawal as the highest form of self-care.

## *A Question For Parents And Caregivers*

The question is not whether children will face discomfort, because they will. The question is whether they will be taught how to remain present through it. Families that teach staying do not eliminate conflict. They create adults capable of navigating it.

In the final chapter, we will examine when separation is necessary—and how to discern the difference between protective distance and avoidant disconnection.

*"If all we teach our children is how to leave, we rob them of the resilience required to build what lasts."*

-Coach Venus

# CHAPTER 12:

## When Separation Is Necessary, And When It's Not

Not all distance is avoidance.
Not all separation is abandonment.

Some relationships are genuinely unsafe. Some patterns are irreparable without significant intervention. Some distance is not only appropriate, but also essential.

The challenge is not acknowledging this truth.
The challenge is discerning when it applies.

### *When Separation Is Necessary*

Separation is warranted when there is ongoing harm that cannot be mitigated through conversation, boundaries, or accountability. This includes patterns of abuse, chronic manipulation, addiction that compromises safety, or persistent violations of clearly stated limits.

In these cases, distance is not punishment, it is protection.

Necessary separation is characterized by clarity. The reasons are articulated. The boundaries are specific. The decision is grounded in reality rather than reactivity.

Even then, separation is not taken lightly. It is often accompanied by grief, reflection, and, where possible, support.

Protection does not require cruelty.
Distance does not require dehumanization.

## *When Separation Becomes Avoidance*

Separation becomes avoidant when it is used to escape discomfort rather than danger. When it replaces communication instead of following failed attempts at repair. When it is enacted suddenly, without explanation, and framed as irreversible.

### *Avoidant separation often carries these markers:*

- Vague accusations without specificity.

- Refusal to engage in dialogue.

- Use of labels instead of behaviors.

- Permanence declared in moments of emotional intensity.

- Moral certainty without reflection.

In these cases, distance does not resolve conflict, it freezes it.

## *Discernment Requires Honesty*

Discernment begins with honest self-examination.

### *Before choosing permanent distance, it is worth asking:*

- Have I clearly named specific behaviors and impacts?

- Have I invited accountability and allowed response?

- Have I tolerated discomfort long enough to seek understanding?

- Am I seeking protection, or control?

- Am I open to repair if conditions change?

These questions are not meant to pressure reconciliation. They are meant to clarify motivation.

## *The Role Of Accountability*

Accountability is the hinge between protection and avoidance.

When separation includes accountability, on both sides, it remains relationally grounded, even if contact is limited. When accountability is absent, separation becomes unilateral and brittle. Healthy distance leaves the door unlocked, even if it remains closed for a time. Avoidant distance bolts the door and throws away the key.

## *Reconsidering Permanence*

One of the most consequential features of modern estrangement is its insistence on permanence. Decisions made in moments of emotional upheaval are framed as final, beyond reconsideration.

But human beings evolve. Insight deepens. Circumstances change. Declaring permanence prematurely denies this reality.

Discernment allows for reassessment. It acknowledges that boundaries can shift as understanding grows, and that repair is sometimes possible long after rupture.

## *A Different Measure Of Strength*

Strength is often equated with decisiveness and finality.

But  relational strength looks different.

*It looks like:*

- Humility without self-erasure.

- Boundaries without ultimatums.

- Distance without demonization.

- Accountability without annihilation.

- Courage to revisit decisions when wisdom expands.

Strength is not proven by how cleanly one cuts people off. It is revealed by how thoughtfully one handles complexity.

## For Parents Who Are Waiting

To parents carrying the ache of estrangement: your grief is real. Your confusion is understandable. Your longing for clarity and connection is not weakness.

You are allowed to hold boundaries of your own. You are allowed to refuse narratives that require your erasure. You are allowed to hope without chasing, to remain open without abandoning yourself.

Waiting does not mean surrendering dignity.

## For Adult Children Who Are Certain

Certainty can feel stabilizing, but it is not the same as peace. Before hardening distance into permanence, consider whether your certainty leaves room for growth, yours or theirs.

Healing is not threatened by conversation.
Boundaries are not weakened by discernment.

Distance chosen wisely remains flexible. Distance chosen defensively does not.

## *A Final Invitation*

This book is not an argument against boundaries. It is an invitation to maturity. It asks that we reclaim accountability alongside autonomy, endurance alongside self-care, and discernment alongside empowerment.

Families will never be perfect. But they do not have to be disposable.

The work is not choosing sides.
The work is choosing wisdom.

And wisdom rarely rushes to cut people off.

*"Discernment is knowing when distance is healing and when it's just hiding. Wisdom asks not if you can walk away, but if you must."*

-Coach Venus

# VIGNETTE

## When Visibility Saves Lives

When **Oprah Winfrey** spoke publicly about family estrangement, the response was immediate. Articles followed. Conversations erupted. People who had never spoken aloud about their families finally found language for what they had been carrying in silence.

For many, it felt like a sudden revelation.
For others, it felt painfully overdue.

Parental estrangement did not begin when a celebrity named it. It has existed quietly for decades, across generations, cultures, and countries; often hidden beneath shame, confusion, and self-blame. What public figures bring is not truth itself, but permission: permission to speak without immediately being dismissed, blamed, or reduced to a stereotype.

That permission matters more than most people realize.

Estrangement is not only a relational rupture. For many parents, it is an existential one. It strips identity, meaning, and purpose from people who have spent their lives giving, often imperfectly, often without guidance, but sincerely. It leaves grief without ritual, pain without witnesses, and questions without answers.

There was a time when the weight of that silence nearly broke me.

Before I had understanding, before I had language, before I knew this was a global pattern and not a personal failure, I felt hopeless. I replayed every sacrifice I had ever made for my children: the sleepless nights, the moments of exhaustion, the tears shed in private when I didn't know the way but kept going anyway. I remembered the work that no one sees, the labor that is messy and thankless, the love that continues even when it is no longer returned.

Without my support system, without my aunt Ivy, my "unpaid therapist," my steady anchor, I would not be here. Silence is dangerous when pain has nowhere to land. Hopelessness grows when suffering has no name and no mirror.

My own story did not begin with ideal conditions. My mother left me when I was thirteen. She was present only intermittently for a few years of my life. I did not grow up with a blueprint. I did not know better for a long time. And yet, when I learned better, I did better. I tried to teach better. I tried to break what I inherited rather than pass it on.

***That context matters.***

Many parents who are now estranged were learning as they went; parenting while healing, loving while surviving, choosing differently without ever having been shown how. The expectation that they should have been perfect, without having been protected or guided themselves, is both unrealistic and deeply unfair.

When estrangement happens without explanation or dialogue, it can push parents into dangerous emotional territory. Despair thrives in isolation. Silence convinces people that their pain is illegitimate, that their lives no longer matter, that their contributions have been erased.

***This is why visibility saves lives.***

Not because celebrities create credibility, but because they crack open conversations that have been sealed shut. They help people realize they are not alone. And sometimes, realizing you are not alone is the difference between giving up and holding on one more day.

This book exists in that space. Not to assign blame. Not to center bitterness. But to keep people alive: emotionally, relationally, and spiritually. It exists because silence nearly cost me my life, and because too many parents are still sitting alone, believing their grief disqualifies them from dignity.

I am no longer explaining myself to earn worth.
I am no longer shrinking to preserve access.
I am now re-teaching people how to treat me.

That, too, is healing.

*"Sometimes the only thing keeping someone alive is the hope that someone still sees them. Visibility is ministry when silence feels like death."*

-Coach Venus

# VIGNETTE

## What Parents Are Not Allowed To Say

We are the parents who do not know how to explain our grief without sounding guilty.

We are the parents who have learned to lower our voices when we speak of our children, because saying their names out loud invites judgment we do not have the strength to carry.

We are told there must be a reason.
We are told to look inward.
We are told to accept silence as consequence.

What we are rarely asked is how we are surviving it.

We loved each other imperfectly, yes, but we loved each other relentlessly. We showed up tired. We showed up unsure. We showed up without road maps, without examples, without having been parented well ourselves. We did the best we could with what we knew at the time, and when we learned better, many of us tried to do better.

That part is often erased.

We remember the nights no one else saw: the worry, the fear, the prayer, the calculations we made just to keep going. We remember choosing our children over ourselves again and again, even when we were breaking quietly inside.

And now, we are expected to disappear gracefully.

We are told that asking questions is manipulation. That wanting explanation is entitlement. That our pain is evidence of our failure rather than proof of our humanity.

We are expected to grieve privately, indefinitely, and without protest.

**There is no space for us to say:**
*I am confused.*
*I am hurting.*
*I do not understand what I did that warrants erasure.*

There is no language for loving someone you are not allowed to speak to. There is no script for carrying pride and grief in the same body. There is no public permission to say, *I miss my child*, without being told that silence is what healing looks like now.

*So, we wait.*

We wait for clarity that may never come.
We wait for time to soften what distance hardened.
We wait while birthdays pass, milestones happen without us, and life continues in fragments we are not allowed to witness.

Waiting is not passive. It is active endurance.

We are not asking to be excused from accountability. We are asking to be included in the conversation. We do not demand agreement. We are asking for dignity. We are not seeking control. We are seeking understanding.

We are still here.
Still loving.
Still remembering.

Even in silence, we are carrying the weight of relationships that mattered enough to grieve.

# VIGNETTE

## What The Silence Doesn't Say

I tell myself this is what I needed.
Distance. Space. Quiet.

At first, it felt like relief; like exhaling after holding my breath for years. No more tension. No more explanation. No more feeling misunderstood in rooms where I was supposed to feel safe.

I told myself I was choosing peace.

And maybe I was.
At least, that's what it felt like in the beginning.

But silence is not empty. It fills itself with questions.

I replay conversations, not the loud ones, but the ordinary ones. The moments that didn't feel dangerous, just disappointing. The times I wanted to be seen differently and didn't know how to say it. The moments I expected them to understand without having to explain myself.

I wonder now if I asked for too much, or if I asked for it the wrong way.

# VENUS CHANDLER

I know what I feel. I'm certain of that.
What I'm less certain of is what my feelings mean.

Sometimes I tell myself that if they really loved me, they would already know. Other times, I wonder if I expected them to read language that I never taught them. I wanted change, but I don't know if I ever said what change would look like.

It's easier to say they were unsafe than to admit I didn't know how to stay when things got hard.

I don't miss the conflict.
But I miss parts of them.

I miss being known without explanation. I miss history. I miss the way they understood my silences before I learned how to name them myself. I miss the version of myself that existed before everything became a boundary.

I don't talk about that part out loud.

In public, my certainty is clean.
In private, it is quieter.

I wonder sometimes if cutting off was strength, or if it was the only tool I had at the time. I wonder if distance healed me, or if it simply stopped the noise long enough for me not to notice what I lost. I tell myself I don't owe anyone access. That may be true, but I still carry questions I never asked.

I don't know what reconciliation would require. I don't know if I'm ready for it, or if I'm afraid that reopening the door would mean admitting I didn't have all the answers after all.

So, I stay where I am.
Certain enough to remain distant.
Uncertain enough to feel the absence.

# CUT OFF

I am not the villain.
They are not the monster.

We are people who did not know how to meet each other in the middle, and who learned to survive by choosing different sides of silence.

*"Silence is not always healing. Sometimes it's a prison, where all the unspoken pain becomes a legacy no one ever meant to leave behind."*

-Coach Venus

# FINAL THOUGHTS

## What We Choose To Carry Forward

Estrangement did not begin as cruelty.
It began as a response to pain.

But pain left unexamined hardens. Silence unchallenged becomes policy. And distance chosen without discernment does not heal, it merely delays the reckoning.

Families are not disposable because they are imperfect. Parents are not irredeemable because they are human. Adult children are not weak because they struggle to name what hurts. But when we replace conversation with cancellation, accountability with certainty, and endurance with escape, we lose something far greater than contact; we lose the capacity to grow together.

Boundaries were never meant to end relationship. They were meant to make relationships possible. Healing is not proven by how cleanly we cut people off. It is revealed by how honestly we examine ourselves, how responsibly we name harm, and how courageously we remain open to repair where repair is possible.

Some separations are necessary.
Some distances are protective.

But permanence should never be declared in moments of emotional intensity, and silence should never be mistaken for strength.

This book does not ask you to tolerate harm.
It asks you to tolerate complexity.

It asks parents to hold accountability without erasure.
It asks adult children to hold autonomy without abandonment.
It asks families to remember that disagreement is not danger, discomfort is not abuse, and growth does not happen without friction.

What we are witnessing is not simply a breakdown of families, it is a breakdown of relational maturity. And that breakdown has consequences that echo far beyond individual households.

The question is not who is right.
The question is who is willing to stay human.

Because the future of family is not determined by who leaves first, but by who is brave enough to choose discernment over certainty, responsibility over righteousness, and connection over control.

What we choose to carry forward will shape generations.

*Choose wisely.*

# *A Letter To My Children*

My children and my grandchildren,

I am writing this letter once: fully, honestly, and with love, so my heart can be at rest, and my words can stand where my presence has not always been allowed.

I want you to know first and without condition: I love you all the same. Nothing has ever changed that, and nothing ever will.

I ask your forgiveness for my part in our story. For what I did not know at the time. For the ways I loved before I understood how to implement healthy boundaries. I now see that my lack of understanding, my desire to give, fix, and hold everything together contributed to pain rather than protection. When you don't know better, you can't do better. And when I learned better, I tried to do better.

*I own that.*

I am sorry for the confusion my growth may have caused. I am sorry for the moments I did not understand how to love in ways that honored both you and me. I am sorry for the ways my learning came later than it should have.

At the same time, I want to be clear: lovingly and respectfully. My boundaries are now in place, and they will remain. Not as walls, but as structure. Not as punishment, but as protection: for all of us. I will not abandon myself to preserve access, and I will not shrink to prove my love. My boundaries are part of my healing, and they allow me to love from a place of truth.

My doors will always be open.
Open does not mean chasing.
Open does not mean erasing myself.
Open means available, willing, and grounded.

I pray for reconciliation. I pray for understanding. I pray for unity; not forced, not rushed, not demanded, but rooted in honesty and mutual respect. If that day never comes, I want you to know this as well: I am at peace. Not because I stopped caring, but because I learned how to hold love without losing myself.

To my grandchildren: especially those I do not yet know. I pray that you find your own voices. I pray that one day you feel safe enough, strong enough, and curious enough to ask questions. To come to me not with fear, but with openness. To seek understanding of my "why," not through silence or assumptions, but through conversation.

I am here for that.

I have always been here.

This letter is not a door closing. It is a door standing open, without expectation, without pressure, and without conditions. It is my final apology, my full accountability, and my lasting love, all in one place.

I release the rest to God, to time, and to whatever healing each of you must walk in your own way.

I love you.
I always have.
I always will.

# CUT OFF

With love and peace,
Mom / Gana
Venus

# VENUS CHANDLER

## ABOUT THE AUTHOR

# VENUS CHANDLER

Venus, originally from Akron, Ohio, now resides in Los Angeles, California. She is a proud mother of three and grandmother to five.

With a professional career spanning 36 years in nursing, Venus has dedicated her life to serving others in various medical facilities, including Lynwood Healthcare Center, Los Angeles Community Hospital, and Bay Vista. She has spent the last nine years as a Nurse Manager at Lighthouse Healthcare Center.

# VENUS CHANDLER

Venus is a published, number 1 best-selling international author, speaker, life coach, and advocate for survivors of childhood trauma. In 2016, she discovered her true purpose—advocating for women and girls, helping them reclaim their power, purpose, and voice. Once she realized her destiny, she acted, committing herself to uplifting others.

Since then, Venus has embraced her calling, moving freely in the plan God has for her life. She launched her own business, *Kintsugi Transformations Life Coaching Services*, with the goal of helping women develop healthy minds, which she believes are essential for building strong, healthy communities.

**Her motto:** *"We are strength in numbers!"*

Venus is also the author of her autobiography, *A Silent Scream: My Story, My Truth,* in which she shares her journey of overcoming obstacles and pursuing her dreams. She is living proof that with determination, anyone can discover their purpose and achieve their goals, one step at a time.

# MORE BOOKS BY THE AUTHOR

The darkness in her eye represents her past. The light in her eye represents her future. The tear on her face represents the pain she endured. The story represents her freedom and healing. Silent No More is an anthology about childhood trauma. The authors are women who experienced horrific abuse and mistreatment when they should have been protected & cherished. They were violated as minors. They were threatened to keep it secret and forced to keep quiet. Featuring Anjanette Robinson, Brandi Marsh, Carra Braxton, Danniel S. Withers, Jaynel Jones, LaLisa Morgan, Lucretia Y. Hayes, Melanie Rossum, Melissa McGill, Porshe Williams, Tanya DeFreitas, and Vernita Edwards, with a bonus by Terry Chandler. As adults, these women are reclaiming their liberty and victory by telling their truth and they are Silent No More! It's not an easy read, but it was not an easy journey getting to the place of being able to share what they experienced.

# VENUS CHANDLER

The story within *A Silent Scream* is far from unique, yet it resonates with countless others who have walked a similar path. In writing this book, Venus Chandler brings attention to the often-overlooked struggles that many face daily. Themes of molestation, rape, addiction, money, and prostitution shaped her journey, but they do not define her. Venus is not a victim of her past; she is a survivor.

This book is written for every broken soul, especially for women who have endured unimaginable trials. It reaches out to those who have wrestled with thoughts of suicide, harbored anger, or dealt with the weight of PTSD. *A Silent Scream* is dedicated to anyone who has had their innocence stolen, suffered sexual abuse, or been harmed by those they trusted to protect them.

Venus Chandler invites readers to reclaim themselves and find their voice. In *A Silent Scream*, she extends permission to release the grip of the past. With each breath and each moment of hope, this book encourages readers to dream again and to become the person they have always longed to be.

# CUT OFF

Courage.

This is what it takes to pick up the pieces of a shattered heart. Although challenging, these women took a fearless leap and answered the call. It was a call to healing, restoration and trust in God.

Walk with us beyond the echoes of a shattered heart onto the path of healing and redemption.

Courage.

This is what it takes to pick up the pieces of a shattered heart. Although challenging, these women took a fearless leap and answered the call. It was a call to healing and restoration.

Join Coach Venus Chandler and four other courageous women who walk beyond the echoes of a shattered heart onto the path of healing and redemption.

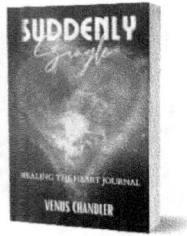

Writing is therapy, and Coach Venus is here to help you mend your healing heart through writing.

This journal is designed to accompany the book: SUDDENLY Single-An Anthology. Coach Venus compiled this journal in hopes that you will take your journey a step further by writing your pain and tears away.

Receive the healing your heart needs and watch breakthroughs come on the other side!

Brutal Courage is an anthology about cruel strength and the women who possess it. In this book, you will follow the journey of 12 women who have experienced life-changing moments that reshaped their world forever. They had to be strong, courageous, and fearless.

It was often a matter of life or death. Their will to live was stronger than they were at times, and that helped them get through. Featuring Anthologist and Lead Author, Tanya DeFreitas, along with Anjanette Robinson, Audrea V. Heard, Barbara Thomas, Cheriese Foster, Jaynel Jones, Keci Monique, Lupe Duran, Melissa Brown, Melissa McGill, Savannah West, and Venus Chandler. They are bold, brave, and united as they join forces to tell their stories.

These are stories of tragedy & triumph, victimization & victory. The truth is revealed, secrets are exposed; It gets real, it gets raw, it gets BRUTAL!